D1712537

Spotlight on the 13 Colonies
Birth of a Nation

★ ★ ★ ★ ★ ★ ★ ★ ★ ★ ★ ★

THE
LOST COLONY OF
ROANOKE

Caitie McAneney

PowerKiDS press™

NEW YORK

Published in 2016 by The Rosen Publishing Group, Inc.
29 East 21st Street, New York, NY 10010

Editor: Caitie McAneney
Book Design: Andrea Davison-Bartolotta

Photo Credits: Cover, p. 17 Stock Montage/Getty Images; pp. 4–5, 10–11 North Wind Picture Archives; p. 6
Zack Frank/Shutterstock.com; pp. 7, 13 Hulton Archive/Getty Images; p. 9 Theodore de Bry/Getty Images;
pp. 14–15 DEA Picture Library/DeAgostini/Getty Images; p. 19 (main) courtesy of Library of Congress; p. 19
(inset) Jeffrey Phelps/Getty Images; p. 20 courtesy of National Park Service; p. 21 Martin Ruegner/Getty Images;
p. 22 Dennis K. Johnson/Getty Images.

Cataloging-in-Publication Data

McAneney, Caitie.
The lost colony of Roanoke / by Caitie McAneney.
p. cm. — (Spotlight on the 13 colonies: Birth of a nation)
Includes index.
ISBN 978-1-4994-0596-5 (pbk.)
ISBN 978-1-4994-0601-6 (6 pack)
ISBN 978-1-4994-0600-9 (library binding)
1. Roanoke Colony — Juvenile literature. 2. Roanoke Island (N.C.) — History — Juvenile literature. I. McAneney,
Caitlin II. Title.
F229.M138 2016
975.6'175—d23

Manufactured in the United States of America

CPSIA Compliance Information: Batch #WS15PK: For further information contact Rosen Publishing, New York, New York at 1-800-237-9932.

Contents

An Ocean Away

In the 1500s, England was a small nation that wanted to **expand** its trade. European nations such as France and Spain had already sent explorers across the Atlantic Ocean to chart the Americas and discover new **resources**. They called the Americas the New World. By the 1580s, England, led by Queen Elizabeth I, wanted its chance at a piece of the New World. This mysterious place was said to offer valuable resources and riches, such as furs, silver, and even gold.

An adventurer named Sir Walter Raleigh was ready to take on the challenge of exploring and settling the New World for England. He funded the **expeditions** that explored and built a settlement on Roanoke Island. This island is off the coast of what is now North Carolina. Settlers on Roanoke were faced with many challenges in their short time on the island. After its failure, Roanoke became known as the scene of one of the greatest mysteries of all time.

Within three years, all settlers on Roanoke disappeared without a trace. This mystery has left historians baffled. What happened to the settlers? Did they starve? Did native tribes attack them? Researchers hope to find answers soon.

Exploring Roanoke Island

In all, three groups of Englishmen arrived at Roanoke Island. Raleigh had received a royal patent that said he could settle land for England. In 1584, his first expedition left England on two ships captained by Philip Amadas and Arthur Barlowe. The expedition's purpose was reconnaissance, or observation of a region meant to gather information. After exploring the East Coast of North America, they claimed a part of it for England. They named it Virginia.

The expedition found an island that seemed to be a good location for a colony. They met the Roanoke Indians and named the island after them. At first, these natives were friendly and offered **hospitality** to the new arrivals. Amadas and Barlowe even took two high-ranking Indians, named Manteo and Wanchese, back to England. The expedition made sure to boast of the great wonders of the New World. Raleigh began making plans for more people to travel there.

Fort Raleigh National Historic Site forest

The Roanoke tribe was one of the many Algonquian-speaking tribes that existed along the East Coast. In this picture, Englishmen barter, or trade, with natives on Roanoke Island.

The Second Expedition

The second group to arrive on Roanoke Island was there on a scientific and military mission. There were 108 men on this trip, led by Sir Richard Grenville and Colonel Ralph Lane. The group arrived on July 3, 1585, to study the available resources.

Grenville returned to England in August, and the expedition explored the mainland near Roanoke Island. They recorded what they saw, and an artist named John White painted pictures of unfamiliar plants and animals, as well as Native Americans and their homes, villages, and ways of life.

Unlike the first group, the second group of Englishmen didn't get along with natives. Native Americans died from illnesses the English brought, which caused **tension**. The English burned a village and killed a Roanoke Indian leader, which made tensions even worse. By the end of the year, the Englishmen were suffering from lack of supplies and food. In June 1586, they **abandoned** Roanoke with a visiting explorer, Sir Francis Drake. Grenville returned in July, not realizing the men had left. When he set sail for England again, he left behind 15 men with supplies for a year.

Despite the dangerous experience of the expedition, Thomas Hariot wrote *A Briefe and True Report of the New Found Land of Virginia* in 1590. This book told of all the great things the New World had to offer. The report was complete with engravings by Theodor de Bry based on paintings John White had made of the creatures and resources of America. This engraving of a Secoton village has had coloring added by hand.

Stuck on the Island

Even though the last group abandoned Roanoke, there were still Englishmen who wanted to settle in the New World. Another group of colonists set sail in May 1587. This time, there were women and children, which meant it was more than just a mission. It was a serious attempt at making a colony.

There were about 110 colonists in the group, and they had to pay for their own trip. In return, each man would get 500 acres (203 ha) of land and a voice in the colonial government. John White, the artist, was named as the governor.

The colonists were headed for Chesapeake Bay, which they believed had better land than Roanoke and friendlier Indians. There, they would build the "Cittie of Relagh," or "City of Raleigh." However, Raleigh ordered White to stop at Roanoke Island first to see what had happened to the 15 men Grenville had left behind. When they arrived on July 22, 1587, the colonists found only abandoned houses and the bones of one of Grenville's soldiers. They also found that relations with tribes were no longer friendly.

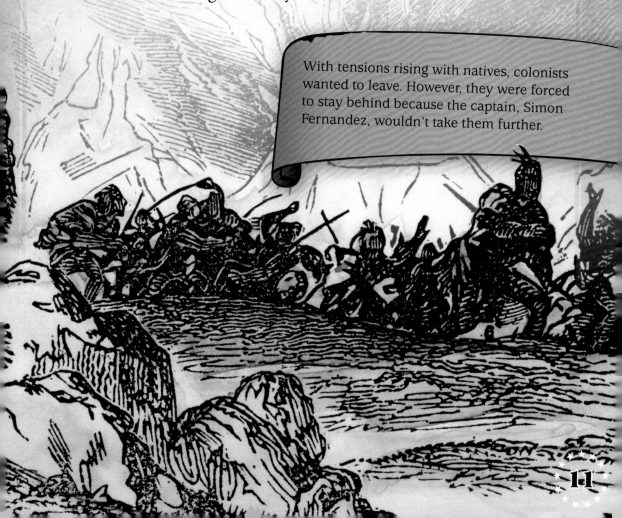

With tensions rising with natives, colonists wanted to leave. However, they were forced to stay behind because the captain, Simon Fernandez, wouldn't take them further.

Building New Roanoke

Even though they wanted to leave, the colonists started to settle Roanoke, probably near Fort Raleigh, which was left by Grenville's soldiers. They rebuilt old houses left by the second group and started building new homes. On August 18, 1587, John White's daughter gave birth to the first English child born in the New World, named Virginia Dare.

Within weeks, supplies were running low. The colonists still hoped to move to Chesapeake Bay, but couldn't make the move without supplies. They knew the dangers of staying in Roanoke. Indian attacks, food shortage, and illnesses were constant worries. The colonists were stuck in a strange land with few **allies** and few resources.

John White knew he had to return to England to get supplies. He left on August 27, with a promise that he'd be back soon. The colonists told White that if he didn't return soon, they'd carve their **destination** on a tree. If they left because of an Indian attack, they'd add a special cross symbol.

This painting shows the **baptism** of Virginia Dare, the first English child born in America. Her birth was a joyous moment in an otherwise difficult time for the colonists.

Three Years Gone

White returned to England, but met many challenges before he could leave for Roanoke again. When he arrived in England, tension was brewing between England and Spain, and reports spread that there might be a Spanish attack. In July 1588, the Spanish Armada, sent by King Philip II of Spain, attacked England. An armada is a fleet of warships, and this one was powerful. There were over 100 ships and about 30,000 men. King Philip wanted to take Queen Elizabeth's throne and make Protestant England into a Roman Catholic country, like Spain.

Unfortunately for White, the beginning of war between England and Spain meant his stranded colony was unimportant. The English needed all the ships and supplies they could find, so they couldn't give any to White to return to Roanoke. White could do nothing until the war was over. It took three years until White could find a ship to sail back to Roanoke.

This picture shows the British navy fighting off the advancing Spanish Armada.

An Abandoned Village

John White finally returned to Roanoke Island three years after he'd left. However, the colonists were nowhere to be found. They left behind a few scattered belongings, but the houses had been taken down.

True to their word, the colonists had left a message about their destination. The first message was the word "Cro" written on a tree near shore. That was John White's first clue to what happened. Then, as he was searching the abandoned village, White found a **palisade** with the word "Croatoan." There was no cross near it, so he figured it wasn't an Indian attack. White thought this was a message from the colonists meaning that they had gone to stay with the Croatoan Indians on Hatteras Island.

However, White never reached the Croatoans on their island. A terrible storm made it too risky to **navigate** the choppy waters. Instead, White had to abandon Roanoke and sail back to England. He never saw his daughter or his granddaughter again. Roanoke became known as the "Lost Colony," and its people were never found.

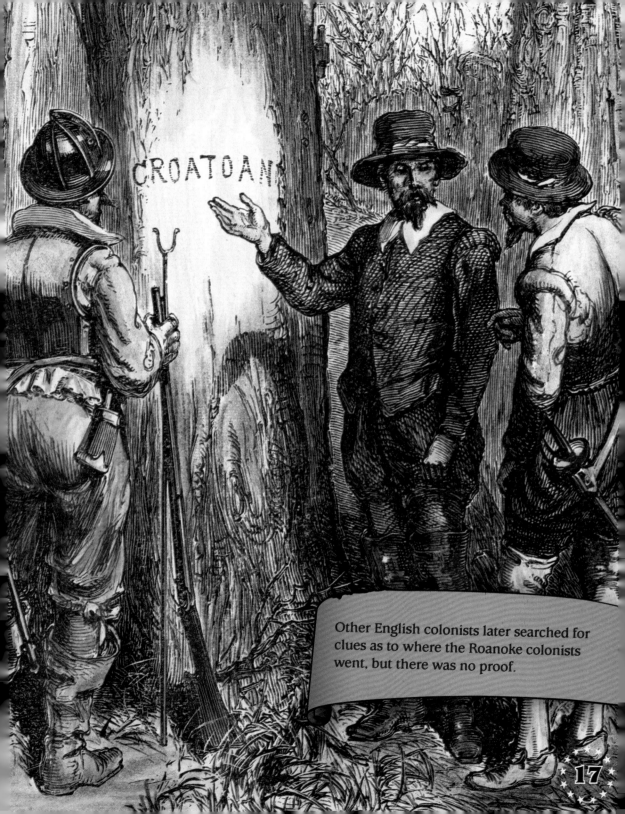

Other English colonists later searched for clues as to where the Roanoke colonists went, but there was no proof.

Roanoke Theories and Legends

From the beginning, there were many **theories** and **legends** about what had happened to the colonists. Some believed the colonists died from disease. There were illnesses in the New World that the colonists weren't used to, such as **malaria**. Others believed the colonists were attacked by natives.

Many believed the colonists left Roanoke for a new place. A major theory was that the colonists abandoned Roanoke and traveled to Croatoan Island, because of their message on the palisade. Today, some **archaeologists** suggest they may have traveled in another direction to a friendly tribe that might have adopted them.

There were reports that some of the colonists were still alive until around 1610. Settlers to Jamestown were given the task of trying to find the colonists or discover what happened. There were reports that some of the lost colonists lived with a tribe in Chesapeake Bay for a while. The colonists might have split up into smaller groups to have more luck for survival.

Virginia Dare

One legend tells the fictional story of what might have happened to Virginia Dare. Legend has it that natives attacked the Roanoke colony, but the Croatoan tribe saved Virginia Dare. She was raised in the tribe, but a medicine man turned her into a white deer. That's why Virginia Dare is sometimes called the White Doe.

Investigating Roanoke

Today, we have new ideas as to what might have happened to the colonists at Roanoke. In 1998, archaeologists studied tree rings near Roanoke and found that there was a severe **drought** between 1587 and 1589, the time when the colonists were stranded.

Today's archaeologists have new technology to uncover history's mysteries. In 2012, scientists looked at a map by John White and noticed there was a patch on it. Using special lights, they found a symbol underneath that might have stood for a fort. The fort would have been 50 miles (80 km) away, in an area near the small tribal town of Mettaquem.

Fort Raleigh archaeological dig, 2009

Archaeologists traveled to that location to use ground-penetrating radar (GPR). GPR sends radio waves into the ground, where they bounce off objects. Archaeologists found a buried structure and a fence, meaning colonists could have been there. However, more research will have to be done because it's not clear what the buildings were, when they were made, or who made them.

What can tree rings tell us? A tree gains one new ring in its trunk every year. The bigger the space between rings, the more the tree grew, and the better the growing conditions. The space between rings was very close between 1587 and 1589, which shows that growing conditions were poor.

Roanoke Today

Where exactly did the colonists settle on Roanoke Island? Archaeologists aren't completely sure. **Artifacts** found on the island give archaeologists clues, but no one knows where the actual houses once stood.

Roanoke was settled again in the mid-1600s. During the Civil War, it was used as a freedmen's colony, which is a place where ex-slaves could live and work. Roanoke Island was the site of a major victory for the North when they captured the island in 1862.

Today, Roanoke Island is part of North Carolina. It has two towns, Wanchese and Manteo. The island hosts Fort Raleigh, a national historic site that protects and preserves areas where the first colonists likely settled. There's also an outdoor play at the Waterside Theater called *The Lost Colony* that's been performed since 1937. It tells the story of the lost colonists and keeps their memory alive. What happened to the colonists at Roanoke? It's a mystery. But maybe someday—armed with new technology and clues—we'll find the answer.

Waterside Theater

Glossary

abandon: To leave.

ally: One of two or more people or groups who work together.

archaeologist: Someone who studies the remains of peoples from the past to understand how they lived.

artifact: An object remaining from a past period.

baptism: A Christian ritual involving blessed water that admits someone into the Christian community.

destination: A place that is set for the end of a journey.

drought: A long period of very dry weather.

expand: To grow larger.

expedition: A trip made for a certain purpose.

hospitality: The welcoming of guests or strangers into one's home or territory.

legend: A story handed down from the past.

malaria: A disease involving a high fever that's passed from one person to another by mosquito bites.

navigate: To find one's way.

palisade: A strong fence for defense.

resource: Something that can be used.

tension: A state of unrest or opposition between individuals or groups.

theory: An idea that tries to explain something.

Index

Primary Source List

p. 9
The Village of Secoton. Created by Theodor de Bry. Hand-colored engraving. Based on a watercolor painting by John White. Included in *A Briefe and True Report of the New Found Land of Virginia* by Thomas Hariot, published in London, England, in 1590.

pp. 14/15
Launch of Fireships Against the Spanish Armada. Created by unknown Netherlandish artist. Oil on canvas. ca. 1590. Now kept at the National Maritime Museum, Greenwich, London, United Kingdom.

Websites

Due to the changing nature of Internet links, PowerKids Press has developed an online list of websites related to the subject of this book. This site is updated regularly. Please use this link to access the list: www.powerkidslinks.com/s13c/roan